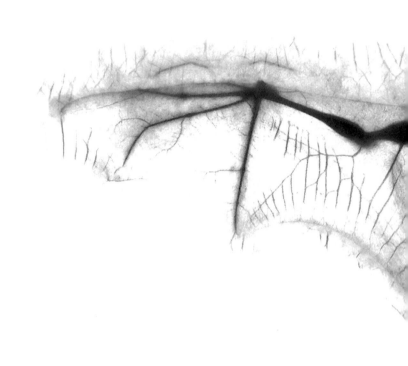

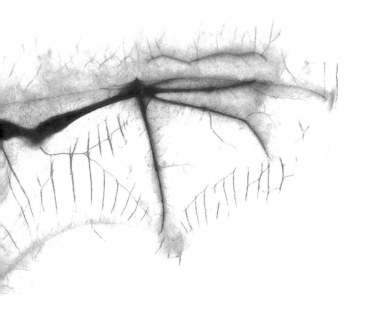

DRÁPA

DRÁPA
The Slaying

Gerður Kristný
translated by Rory McTurk

with an introduction by
Guðni Elísson &
Alda Björk Valdimarsdóttir

2018

Published by Arc Publications
Nanholme Mill, Shaw Wood Road
Todmorden OL14 6DA, UK
www.arcpublications.co.uk

Design by Tony Ward
Printed by TJ International, Padstow

978 1911469 26 1 (pbk)
978 1911469 27 8 (hbk)
978 1911469 28 5 (ebk)

Illustrations © Alexandra Buhl / Forlagið

Drápa was originally published in 2014 by Forlagið Publishing,
Reykjavík, Iceland, by whose kind permission the Icelandic text is
reproduced in this volume.

The publishers acknowledge the financial assistance of

Bókmenntasjóður
The Icelandic Literature Fund

Contents

When Murder Comes to Town
The Dark Vision of Gerður Kristný

FEMINIST POETRY AND THE FAUST IDEA

What is the Faust idea? According to the German philosopher Friedrich Nietzsche it is simply this: a 'little seamstress is seduced and dishonoured' by the greatest scholar of the times, a man of the world who would not have succeeded in this without the 'assistance of the Devil'. One can almost feel Nietzsche's dismay when he asks in wonder: 'Is this really supposed to be the greatest German "tragic idea", as Germans say it is?'[1] What irks Nietzsche even more is the fact that Goethe feels pity for his 'little seamstress', for as Johann Wolfgang von Goethe (1749-1832) himself once admitted, his 'nature was too conciliatory for real tragedy'.[2] After Gretchen is put to death, she is transported to heaven where she will be united with Faust towards the end of the play's second part.

The Icelandic poet Gerður Kristný does not share Nietzsche's view on what is a fit subject for tragedy, for in the last two decades she has repeatedly told tragic stories of abused women, and her narrative poem *Drápa* or *The*

---

[1] Friedrich Nietzsche: *Human, All Too Human*, trans. R. J. Hollingdale, Cambridge: Cambridge University Press, 1996, p. 340.
[2] *Ibid.*

Slaying is here no exception. In it she tells the story of Gréta Birgisdóttir, who was murdered by her husband Bragi Ólafsson in January 1988. He is the 'boxer' of the tale, and was interviewed by Gerður Kristný ten years after the murder in the very apartment where it had taken place. Bragi claimed the murder was an accident. The couple had been drinking for four days when a physical argument broke out. In the end Bragi strangled Gréta with ropes before going to sleep again. The court documents describe in horrifying detail how Gréta was savagely beaten up and kicked in the head, and how the ropes wrapped round her neck broke her thyroid cartilage, with suffocation as the inevitable result.

Bragi was sentenced to ten years in prison for the murder, but he was in no way out of the glaring limelight. At the time of the interview he was himself recovering from severe knife wounds inflicted by his grandson, who had stabbed him repeatedly in the apartment on Boxing Day in 1997.[3] Four years later, in 2002, Bragi would eventually be stabbed to death by a mentally ill drug user in the very same apartment in which he had hanged his wife in 1988. These repeated acts of violence, which are expounded in the poem, led journalists to name the 'three-storeyed house / of timber' (p. 57) at Klapparstígur 11 'a house of misery'.[4]

---

[3] Gerður Kristný: 'Sé eftir að hafa fæðst!' ['I Regret Having Been Born'], *Séð og heyrt*, 10/1998, pp. 13-14.
[4] See NN: 'Hörmungarhús við Klapparstíg' ['A House of Misery on Klapparstígur'], *DV*, 2 April 2005, pp. 16-17; and Óttar

In the poem *The Slaying* Gerður Kristný builds on her experiences as a journalist and a magazine editor, for in the years between 1994 and 2004 she worked at the Icelandic publishing house Fróði, where she interviewed various criminals who were linked to the Icelandic underworld, convicted murderers and hoodlums. An ongoing theme in those articles and interviews was violence against women, both sexual abuse and assault and battery. Gerður's investigative journalism culminates in her book *Portrait of Daddy. Thelma's Story*,[5] for which she received the Booksellers' Literary Award in 2005 and Iceland's Journalism Award also in 2005.

In *Portrait of Daddy* Gerður Kristný tells the story of Telma Ásdísardóttir (Thelma) who for years was sexually abused, along with her four sisters, by her father and by men in his small circle of paedophiles. Gerður's work played an important part in drawing attention to the unmentionable sexual violence that Icelandic children had for so long suffered in silence. As Gerður herself points out in an interview given after the publication of the book, 'police reports showed that the neighbours knew exactly how he tortured his daughters',[6] but did nothing, possibly because times were different then and people

---

Sveinsson: 'Geðsjúkur afbrotamaður á reynslulausn' ['A Mentally Ill Offender on Probation'], *DV*, 28 September 2002, p. 14.
[5] Gerður Kristný: *Myndin af pabba. Saga Telmu* [Portrait of Daddy. Thelma's Story], Reykjavík: Mál og menning, 2005.
[6] Bergþóra Njála Guðmundsdóttir: 'Skömmin er ekki mín' ['The Shame is Not Mine'], *Tímarit Morgunblaðsins*, 9 October 2005, pp. 10-17, here p. 16.

thought the right to privacy was important. The book was supposed to challenge this kind of attitude, to bring the issue into the forefront of public debate. Or, as Gerður puts it in the same interview: 'If we cannot talk about sexual violence people will continue to act as if it does not exist, and then we cannot hope that the judicial system will respond to these crimes with any vigour, as can be seen by looking at the case against Thelma's father.'[7]

There is a direct link between *Portrait of Daddy* and *The Slaying*, for both works are feminist critiques focusing on the systemic violence that has for so long been directed against women. But *The Slaying* is not the first narrative poem Gerður Kristný has written on the subject. *Bloodhoof* or *Blóðhófnir*, for which Gerður received the Icelandic Literature Prize in 2010, is also a tale about sexual abuse and human trafficking, in which Gerður rewrites the medieval Icelandic poem *Skírnismál* ('Words of Skírnir') from a feminist standpoint. In the original tale, the god Freyr observes from the vantage point of Óðinn's throne the beautiful giantmaiden Gerður at her father's home in Giantland and immediately falls in love with her. He sends his servant Skírnir to woo the maiden on his behalf and Skírnir succeeds in doing so. This poem has long been received as a grand romantic tale, but feminists have in recent years pointed out the underlying violence in Skírnir's proposal, because Gerður the giantmaiden agrees to leave for Asgarður, the home of the gods, only under duress, after threats of mutilation and

---

[7] *Ibid.*

death. It is from the point of view of her namesake that Gerður Kristný writes the poem, stressing the maiden's fear and misery through the whole ordeal. To quote but a few lines from Rory McTurk's English translation: 'Over my head / the sword sang a song / the song of a maiden / who struggles / and dies // her neck decked with a slash [...] I said yes, I would come // and I saw my face, / dead, reflected / in the envoy's sword.'[8]

In her homeland Gerður Kristný is recognized for her attempts to bring trauma and abuse into the forefront of public debate, not only in her professional capacity as a writer and poet, but also through her work as a journalist and editor. It was therefore no surprise when she was selected to give a reading from *Bloodhoof* in October 2010 in front of fifty thousand Icelandic women, who had come together to celebrate the fact that 35 years had passed since the original Women's Holiday in Iceland.[9] In choosing her for this purpose the organizers were honouring Gerður Kristný for being a woman not easily swayed, a woman 'with bone in her nose', to use the Icelandic idiom.

---

[8] Gerður Kristný: *Bloodhoof*, trans. Rory McTurk, Todmorden: Arc Publications, 2012, pp. 46 and 59.
[9] Ingibjörg Dögg Kjartansdóttir: 'Hafnaði fyrsta bónorðinu' ['First Proposal Turned Down'], *DV*, 29 October 2010, pp. 34-36. A detailed account of Gerður Kristný's feminist writings can be found in Alda Björk Valdimarsdóttir and Guðni Elísson: 'Dauðinn og stúlkan: Gerður Kristný og raddir kúgaðra kvenna' ['Death and the Maiden: Gerður Kristný and the Voices of Abused Women'] *Són* 2017 (15), pp. 45-61.

The Slaying is, of course, a poem about a killing, and with Gerður Kristný's work as a journalist in mind we may compare it to modern true crime fiction, such as Vincent Bugliosi's and Curt Gentry's *Helter Skelter. The True Story of The Mason Murders*, and Truman Capote's *In Cold Blood*. Another way of contextualizing the poem would be to suggest links with Scandinavian crime fiction, as Gerður herself has done, arguing in an interview that 'As a matter of fact these are crime poems. After the wave of Nordic crime fiction the time has surely arrived for the Nordic crime poem'.[10] The strong 'sociopolitical insights' of the Scandinavian crime novel, to use an idiom from Barry Forshaw's introduction to his book on the subject, *Death in a Cold Climate*,[11] would here help to make the connection, since *The Slaying* has a moral agenda, but its actual setting also suggests a link to this new subgenre of crime fiction.

As is so often the case with the Nordic crime novel, Gerður Kristný's tale describes punishing winters and long dark winter nights.[12] It opens with a scene from

---

[10] Friðrika Benónýsdóttir: 'Myrkusinn kemur í bæinn' ['The Darcus Comes to Town'], *Fréttablaðið*, 25 October 2014, p. 38.

[11] Barry Forshaw: *Death in a Cold Climate. A Guide to Scandinavian Crime Fiction*, New York: Palgrave Macmillan, 2012, p. 2.

[12] See for example Barry Forshaw's discussion in *Death in a Cold Climate. A Guide to Scandinavian Crime Fiction*, pp. 18 and 133. To illustrate this point it should be enough simply to name the overtly suggestive titles of Icelandic crime fiction in

Reykjavik, with the city bathed in harsh January light and covered in snow, sometimes made brittle and hard by the frost, sometimes reducing visibility to almost nothing:

Snowflakes floated
onto the pavement

The city vanished
overcome by night
into drifting snow (p. 37)

Rabid winds
besieged the town
sent downpours down
to its very core

The winter war
had begun

City-dwellers
ran for shelter (p. 38)

It is an ominous time, a season full of dark forebodings, where the fragments of fallen stars 'point / like

---

English translations, such as Arnaldur Indriðason's *Artic Chill* and *Hypothermia*, Ragnar Jónsson's *Snowblind*, *Nightblind* and *Blackout* (all marketed under the heading 'Dark Iceland') and Yrsa Sigurðardóttir's *The Day is Dark*, to name but a few.

knife-tips upwards / through new-fallen snow' (p. 29) and 'night falls / with the whistling sound // of an axe' (p. 31).

Rory McTurk's translation makes good use of the language which characterizes the Nordic crime genre, but the title choice also suggests to the reader another way of contextualizing the poem. Gerður Kristný's *Drápa* becomes *The Slaying* in the English translation, which is an apt title, incorporating the word *lay*, since this is a narrative poem, a lay, dealing with a murder, the prelude to it and its aftermath: the genre known as 'murder ballad' comes to mind. Gerður herself suggests this comparison in choosing the title *Drápa*. Even though the murder ballad genre is unknown in Icelandic literature, and the word *drápa* simply refers to a long Old Norse poem with refrains, the noun *dráp* also means a killing or a slaughter, and Gerður knowingly exploits this connotation. Thus, through the wordplay, *Drápa* becomes a long narrative poem about a killing, a slaying.

In addition, Gerður Kristný retains the performative implications associated with the composition of a *drápa*, since the Old Norse *drápa* was traditionally delivered at the courts of the Norwegian kings, from the ninth century onwards. It was a heroic poem fit for rulers, and by choosing this name Gerður subtly turns traditional hierarchy upside down in her typical feminist fashion by writing a commemorative poem for a woman who had few advocates while alive, and could never have expected that her story would be transformed into verse. Gerður herself stresses this point in an interview following the publication of *Drápa* in 2015:

> As a journalist, I wrote several articles about young women who had suffered misfortune. Most of them had not survived it. I thought that I would in time forget these stories, but they never left me. As the years passed by these stories kept recurring to me and I felt that it was only fair to those women that I should deliver a *drápa* in their honour, as the poets of old did in front of the Norwegian kings.[13]

But Gerður Kristný's *The Slaying* is not only the story of a crime and its aftermath. We can also glimpse in it another narrative element, belonging to a different but in some cases related genre. In Gerður's poem, as well as in the newspaper account mentioned earlier, the house on Klapparstígur where the murders took place exists in an almost supernatural realm. It is a house of misery, a house of horror, and in Gerður's poem the unnamed heroine of the tale is led there by her suitor, the 'boxer'. She fails to recognize the house – which is situated in the 'Shadow district' (p. 108)[14] – for what it is, a 'bad place',

---

[13] Friðrika Benónýsdóttir: 'Myrkusinn kemur í bæinn' ['The Darcus Comes to Town'], p. 38.

[14] *Drápa or The Slaying* is a topographic poem in the sense that it follows events that take place in an easily recognizable part of Reykjavík. The actual house where the murders took place is located low on the hillside that slopes towards the sea, just north of the city centre, close to Jón Gunnar Árnason's steel sculpture of the 'Sun Voyager' (40) described in the poem, which stands

and is lured in, like so many children and young women in dark fantastic fiction.

At the moment of entry, Gerður Kristný hints at the protagonist's name, Gréta, for the heroine becomes the Gretel of the Hansel and Gretel fairy-tale. The boxer 'stole the crumbs / from your palm / so you lost your way / in the urban forest // If he had walked there / hale and hearty / none would dare enter / that gloomy wood // You paid / no heed / to the house sinking / until too late // The water sprayed / between boards / cascaded in / through windows // You grabbed hold / of the boxer / your hand / a leaf in his palm' (pp. 61-2).

The name Gréta/Gretel brings us to the third name-sake, Gretchen (or Margarete), the ill-fated heroine of Goethe's *Faust*. The connection with her is established through various allusions to the plot of the play. Not only is *The Slaying* the story of a young woman who is led astray by her lover/husband, with her death as the end result; it is also a Faustian tale about a supernatural

---

on a 'stony beach'. The 'Shadow district' is named after a small homestead, the 'Shadow', which stood on the northern shore of what became the town of Reykjavik in the 19th century. Some associated the name wrongly with the squalor and poverty which characterised the neighbourhood early in the 20th century, but in the last two decades it has become 'gentrified', with expensive high-rises lining the shore and casting their long shadows over the vicinity. For the 19th and 20th century history of the district see Árni Óla: 'Úr sögu Reykjavíkur: Skuggahverfi' ['From the History of Reykjavik: The Shadow District'], *Lesbók Morgunblaðsins*, 9 June 1968, pp. 10-11.

agency. The speaker of *The Slaying* is the Devil himself, who bears witness to the events leading up to the murder, and to its aftermath. As in Goethe's play, Mephistopheles takes on the shape of a black dog, and arrives at the start of the poem in midwinter Reykjavik: 'I glided about / in canine form // The breeze stroked / my sleek coat of hair / laid its hand / on my head // Cats vanished / into bushes / rushed behind / dustbins' (p. 35). Towards the middle of *The Slaying* the Devil assumes bat-like form, similar to that given to him in the silent film *Faust* (1926), made by the German director F. W. Murnau and based on Goethe's tale. There Emil Jannings plays Mephistopheles, and early on in the film the viewer sees him hovering over a plague-ridden city like a gigantic bat, much as the Mephistopheles of Kristný's tale does in Reykjavik.[15]

The Devil is a central force in the poem: he is the one telling the tale, and becomes through his own narrative a part of the Reykjavik cityscape, a sinister figure, reflected 'in the street's hoarfrost' (p. 107), a bat-winged demon, whose 'Wings sprout' from his back, 'black sails / pulled tight between / carved peaks' (p. 79), an entity who stays in the background and observes. He admits to having followed the heroine closely, sometimes as 'a dog / tied to a bench', sometimes as 'a man / with hooves / and hat pulled down / onto a swollen face' (p. 68). At times his presence is felt through the sounds so often associated

---

[15] The design of the Icelandic cover is modelled on this image of a batlike demon. When the book is opened two red wings spread out on the back and front covers.

17

with deep winter, for the Devil reminds the reader that: 'It is not a branch / beating against / the corrugated iron / it is me / filing black claws // so that I may / dig myself in / to the heart' (p. 69). Towards the end of the poem, this Mephistopheles finally takes to the air in very much the same way as the Devil does in Eugène Delacroix's (1798-1863) famous 1828 lithograph from *Faust*.[16] His work of narration is done, and so the tale ends with the words: 'I spend / no more days here / than I need / raise myself in flight / vanish into drifting snow' (p. 109).

This supernatural strand is intensified with the arrival of what is called the 'darcus' (p. 44) in Gerður Kristný's poem, the dark circus or carnival the heroine is made to join, with its threatening clowns who kick the feet from under her and stuff her 'into a coffin' (p. 49). It is the 'boxer' who first 'saves' her, raising 'his fists // ravenous wolves / which bolted down / everything in their path // Beasts / reared for slaughter' (p. 52). As the girl enters into a relationship with the boxer, their underworld existence is governed by the rules of the dark carnival, their everyday life is filled with danger and excitement and she becomes the acrobat of his 'company', a tightrope dancer, who will end up falling 'to her death / with the tightrope woven / round her neck // the threads of the fates' (p. 80).

In her descriptions of the 'darcus' Gerður Kristný not only makes use of the fact that Bragi Ólafsson, Gréta's

---

[16] The title of the illustration is 'Méphistophélès dans les airs', or 'Mephistopheles Airborne'.

murderer, had as a young man a short career as a boxer in the United States;[17] she also draws here on fantastic literature of the kind in which the Devil and/or his minions visit a community in the guise of a travelling show or circus. This is an important motif in fantastic literature, but it is also important to note that the boxer is a man of action who does not have the quiet malevolence of Ray Bradbury's Mr Dark in *Something Wicked This Way Comes* (1962), or of the Other Mother of Neil Gaiman's *Coraline* (2002), to name but two modern tales where the dark carnival plays an important role in the plot.[18] Just as important is the fact that the Devil in Gerður's tale is not cast in the role of deceiver and does not partake in the 'show', at least not directly. He is more of a silent witness who can easily enter small garrets during moments of ultimate truth and observe, as he does immediately after the girl's murder, when the boxer has fallen into an alcoholic stupor: 'The boxer / sleeps the sleep / of the unjust // a deep / dreamless sleep // I bend down towards you / so my lips / touch yours' (pp. 82-3).

This is a Devil who has read 'Gréta's' autopsy reports, but who interestingly enough has little access to the fundamental realities of the human condition. He can point

---

[17] Gerður Kristný: 'Sé eftir að hafa fæðst!' ['I Regret Having Been Born'], *Séð og heyrt*, 10/1998, pp. 13-14.

[18] Other contemporary examples that make use of the dark carnival would be Stephen King's *The Dead Zone* (1983), the horror film *Carnival of Souls* (1962) and the TV-series *Carnivale* (2002-2005).

to the girl's final resting place in the cemetery, but can only hope that 'there was / someone beside you / when you awoke' (p. 105) on the other side of the grave. This Devil can push his tongue 'around / the cranial vault' (p. 85) of the victim, but the girl's innermost thoughts at the moment of death remain concealed from him. In this he also diverges from many of the great beguilers of fantastic literature, from Satan in Milton's *Paradise Lost* onwards: demons who have more understanding than he does of the fundamental secrets of human aspirations, and correspondingly little sympathy.

I know
what your head weighed
but do not know
the last thought
which struggled there
or for whom it was meant (p. 86)

I weigh the lungs
in the palms of my hands
inflate them by blowing

then listen to the air
making its escape

Of your little life
there is nothing left (p. 87)

Perhaps it is difficult to gain a clear understanding of *The Slaying* without acknowledging the role of the Devil in the poem, the Devil who indeed narrates the story and remains throughout passive and distant, but is still sympathetic to the victim's plight.

In his book *The Aesthetics of Murder* Joel Black outlines what he calls a 'general typology of the aesthetics of murder', dividing such stories into four categories: two that belong to popular genres and two that can be considered 'high' artistic literary forms. The detective story and the suspense thriller belong to the former pair of categories, focusing as they do on the 'sleuth's deductive brilliance and the helpless victim's terror', while the psychological dramas of authors such as Shakespeare and Dostoyevsky, the third category, keep their attention primarily 'on the murderer's point of view', often dwelling on the murderer's guilt, confession, or self-justification. The fourth category is what Black calls the 'aesthetics of murder', where the events are seen from the standpoint of a fourth party, a 'bystander, who is at once vulnerable and immune to the murderer whose devastation he or she witnesses.' Black argues that through this passivity the spectator will assume the 'role of (feminine) witness or (masculine) voyeur.'[19]

The Devil in Kristný's poem can indeed be viewed as both a witness and a voyeur. He follows the girl around

---

[19] Joel Black: *The Aesthetics of Murder. A Study in Romantic Literature and Contemporary Culture*, Baltimore and London: The Johns Hopkins University Press, 1991, pp. 65-67.

and views her hanging body with a keen interest when he arrives on the scene of the murder – possibly showing something akin to sexual excitement, or the thrill of being 'ravished' by profound problems such as Dr Faustus celebrates in Christopher Marlowe's play. But he also shows sympathy for her plight, hoping that someone has led her over the marshlands in the afterlife and gathered flowers for her: 'a sheaf of spike-rushes / woolly willow / sedge', and expressing the wish that she 'received everything / [she] deserved' (p. 105). It is also important to note that the reader does not witness the actual murder and can only imagine the victim's terror, since he does not know her last thoughts. From the point of view of Black's argument, there is thus nothing 'thrilling' about the girl's death, and Gerður does not give the killer the opportunity to confess his crimes or give his 'reasons' for the murder.

After the boxer awakes from his slumber he remains in the background for the rest of the poem. Gerður Kristný returns to him only once after the murder of Gréta to describe that of the boxer himself fourteen years later, in 2002 (pp. 97-9). This is interesting, because the poet has had ample opportunity to reproduce the boxer's many justifications for what he did, as supplied to her in interviews with him. But we are given no explanations, and we do not know whether or not the boxer regrets his deed. Gerður has probably chosen to resist giving access to his point of view since it would have been at variance with the poem's central purpose, which is to commemorate the victim, not her murderer.

This is especially interesting in that some of the boxer's more memorable comments in the interviews have stayed with Gerður ever since. The boxer considered himself ill-used and misunderstood after his wife's death. According to his own statements he treated Gréta fairly, and 'loved her not only because he was almost twice her age'.[20] He was also, he claimed, her saviour, her knight in shining armour, someone who 'saved her countless times knowingly and killed her only by mistake.' This last phrase was recounted to us by Gerður herself and does not appear in her published interview with Bragi Ólafsson, even though it has stayed with her for almost twenty years.

Gerður also left the killer's statement out of her poem, even though the extraordinary banality of it speaks volumes. This decision perplexed us at first, and we could not resist the temptation to use the quotation as the title of a public lecture given on the poem. For the sentence reveals, in all its simplicity, the tragic lie or misconception that lurks at the heart of many abusive relationships. But that was no doubt the reason for its exclusion from the poem. In quoting this profoundly revealing untruth the poet would have been shifting her focus away from the victim to the perpetrator, and in this poem there is no room for such manoeuvres. The killer remains silent.

This small example illustrates well Gerður Kristný's commitment to her project, which is laid out clearly in *The Slaying*, culminating at the very end of the poem

---

[20] Gerður Kristný: 'Sé eftir að hafa fæðst!' ['I Regret Having Been Born'], p. 13.

with Gréta's name being 'inscribed // in gilded lettering / on a pillow of stone' (p. 93), while her killer rests in an unmarked grave, alongside his relatives: 'His name nowhere inscribed // Such is the fate / of black-hearted men' (p. 101).[21]

THE POETICS AND TRANSLATION OF *THE SLAYING*

Gerður Kristný's poem *Bloodhoof* concludes with the words 'There is my homeland / wrapped in calm of night // steeped in steel-cold ice'.[22] From the very beginning of her career, almost a quarter of a century ago, Gerður's poetic style has in part been modelled on that of the old Icelandic Edda poems, many of which bear in their titles the word-element -*kviða*, or 'lay'. It is a concise, often frugal style, characterised by a certain reservedness of feeling or sparsity of emotion, and by lines woven together with a strong sense of rhythm and alliteration. After the publication of *Ísfrétt*, Gerður Kristný's first volume of poetry, in 1994,[23] one of the reviewers compared her, at the tender age of 24, to the warrior poet and Viking Egill

---

[21] The power of this symbolic juxtaposition is in no way undermined by the fact that Bragi Ólafsson lies in an unmarked grave, since Gerður Kristný carefully selects the information she uses in her poetic account of the events.
[22] Gerður Kristný: *Bloodhoof*, trans. Rory McTurk, pp. 129-130.
[23] Gerður Kristný: *Ísfrétt* [Reports from the Ice], Reykjavík: Mál og menning, 1994.

Skallagrímsson,[24] possibly after Gerður herself admitted in an interview that she was more interested in Old Norse verse forms such as *fornyrðislag* ('old story metre') and *ljóðaháttur* ('chant metre), than in modern poetry.[25] Gerður has continued on this path ever since, both in her choice of subject matter and poetic style.

For this reason it is especially fortunate that Gerður Kristný's translator is Rory McTurk, Professor Emeritus of Icelandic Studies at the University of Leeds, and a specialist in Old as well as Modern Icelandic language and literature. His masterful understanding of Icelandic is evident in his translations of the Old Icelandic texts of *Kormáks saga* and *Droplaugarsona saga* and the contemporary novels of Steinunn Sigurðardóttir. Jenny Jochens argues in a review that McTurk's translations of the stanzas of *Kormáks saga* disprove Bjarni Einarsson's argument that 'no translation can convey an inkling of the sublime beauty of the language'.[26] In another review Joe Allard argues that McTurk's translation of each of these stanzas presents 'a good poem in English which is

---

[24] Hilmar Örn Hilmarsson: 'Brennandi skip og þokuslæður' ['Burning Ships and Mist'], *Eintak*, 28 April 1994, p. 31.

[25] 'Bókin er eins og meðal Eastwood-mynd, það deyja dálítið margir' ['The book is like your average Clint Eastwood film, with one death after another'], *Eintak*, 7 April 1994, p. 28.

[26] Jenny Jochens, review of *The Complete Sagas of Icelanders Including 49 Tales*, ed. by Viðar Hreinsson et al., 5 vols, Reykjavík: Leifur Eiríksson, 1997, in *Journal of English and Germanic Philology* 98 (1999), pp. 284-86, here p. 285.

equivalent in many important respects to the original.'[27] The same attention to detail and keen sense of artistry are revealed in McTurk's translation of Gerður Kristný's other narrative poem, *Bloodhoof*, which Keith Richmond praised in *Tribune Magazine* as follows: 'Rory McTurk, Emeritus Professor of Icelandic Studies at Leeds University, has made a splendid translation of Gerður Kristný's spare modern masterpiece.'[28] The same can be argued in the case of *The Slaying*.

Gréta's poem has now arrived in English. She will not be forgotten in a hurry.

Guðni Elísson & Alda Björk Valdimarsdóttir
University of Iceland

---

[27] Joe Allard, review of *The Complete Sagas of Icelanders Including 49 Tales* (see the previous Note), in *Translation and Literature* 7 (1998), pp. 25-30, here p. 29.
[28] Keith Richmond, review of *Bloodhoof* by Gerður Kristný, trans. Rory McTurk, in *Tribune Magazine*, 25 January 2013, p. 18.

DRÁPA

Stjörnur hafa fallið
úr festingunni
sáldrast yfir götur

Brotin stingast
eins og hnífsoddar
upp úr mjöllinni

Stars have fallen
out of the firmament
bespangling the streets

Their fragments point
like knife-tips upwards
through new-fallen snow

Flugvél brýst
út úr skýjunum

strýkst við
marglit þökin
í miðbænum

An aeroplane
breaks through the clouds

brushing against
the many-coloured roofs
in the heart of town

Í Reykjavík
fellur nóttin
með hvini

eins og öxi

In Reykjavík
night falls
with the whistling sound

of an axe

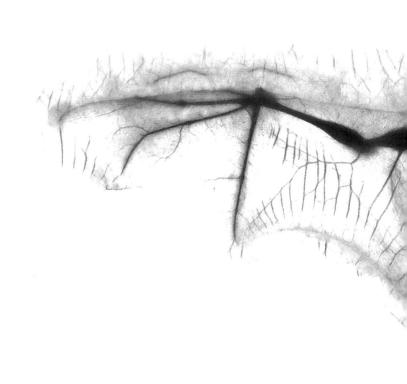

Það var um vetur
kuldinn lagði
lófa yfir heiminn

This was wintertime
the cold cupped the world
in the palm of its hand

Skýin héngu grá
eins og dúfurnar
fiðraðar ufsagrýlur
sem sváfu
undir þakskeggjum

The clouds hung grey
as pigeons
like feathered gargoyles
sleeping
under eaves

Ég leið um
í líki hunds

Golan strauk
snöggan feld
hvíldi hönd
á kolli mínum

Kettir hurfu
inn í runna
hentust bak við
tunnur

I glided about
in canine form

The breeze stroked
my sleek coat of hair
laid its hand
on my head

Cats vanished
into bushes
rushed behind
dustbins

Krossinn
á kirkjuturninum
náði ekki að
rjúfa myrkrið
sem grúfði
yfir húsunum

The cross
on the church tower
could do nothing to break
the darkness louring
over the houses

Snjókorn svifu
niður á stéttina

Borgin
slegin nóttu
hvarf í kóf

Snowflakes floated
onto the pavement

The city vanished
overcome by night
into drifting snow

Bandóðir vindar
sátu um bæinn
sendu hryðjur
ofan í miðja byggð

Vetrarstríðið
var hafið

Borgarbúar
hlupu í skjól

Rabid winds
besieged the town
sent downpours down
to its very core

The winter war
had begun

City-dwellers
ran for shelter

Veturinn tekur
aldrei fanga

Hann leiðir fólk
fyrir næsta horn
þar sem skothríðin bíður

The winter never
takes prisoners

It leads people
round the next corner
into a storm of bullets

Stjörnur rótuðu sér
í gróp sinni

Hlýðinn laumaðist
kvíðinn inn í drauma

Ég vakti þig með hvísli

Stars moved
in their grooves

Anxiety sneaked
meekly into dreams

I awoke you with a whisper

Þú sem fékkst
ekki sofið
klæddir þig
í hvíta peysu

Svartar rósir
fléttuðust
um brjóstið

Fjúk lék
um fætur

You who could
not sleep
put on
a white sweater

Black roses
bedecked
your bosom

Driving snow played
around your feet

Þú halladir
aftur höfdi
greipst snjókornin
med tungunni

Vid Stjörnubíó
voru þau
sölt og brakandi

Hjá hannyrdabúdinni
stingandi hvöss

You tilted
your head back
caught the snowflakes
with your tongue

By the Star cinema
they were
salty and crunchy

By the needlework shop
they were piercingly sharp

Svo sigldu skýin burt
hurfu út á himindjúpið

Norðurljósin
skriðu fram
sveifluðu hölum
um hvolfið
með gneistum

Then the clouds sailed from sight
into heaven's depths

The northern lights
crept forward, scattering
sparks with their tails
round the vault
of heaven

Myrkusinn
var kominn
í bæinn

steypti yfir þig
þéttriðnu tjaldi

The darcus
had come
to town

threw down over you
a close-meshed tent

Trúðar stigu
út á tindrandi stéttina

Nefin
glóandi kýli
runnu á ilminn af
einsemdinni

Þeir slógu
um þig hring

Slógu

Clowns stepped out
onto the glittering pavement

Their noses
glowing carbuncles
caught the scent
of loneliness

They beat their way
into a circle

round you

Gylltir hnappar
kipruðust sem
kattaraugu

Fallbyssukúla
flaug úr pípuhatti

Merki var gefið

Gilded buttons
dwindled
like catseyes

Out of a top hat
flew a cannonball

A sign was given

Trúður spúði eldi
annar keyrði sverð
niður kok sér
þriðji batt
þrjá hnúta
á rauðan klút
stakk upp í ginið
og gleypti

dró stríðsfánann
út um bólgið nef

A clown spat fire
another thrust a sword
down his throat
a third tied
three knots
in a red cloth
stuck it in his jaws
and swallowed

pulled the battle-flag
from his bulging nose

Þeir spörkuðu
undan þér
fótunum

Nötrandi beiðstu
næsta höggs

They kicked
your feet
from under you

Trembling you waited
for the next blow

Trúðarnir
tróðu þér
ofan í kistu

Lyktin
af viði og voða
lamaði

The clowns
stuffed you
into a coffin

The smell
of wood and peril
was paralysing

Djúp naglför
deyjandi manna
greypt í lokið

Trúðarnir
söguðu sér leið
inn í óttann

Deep traces
of dead men's nails
were scratched on the lid

The clowns
sawed their way
into that horror

Sagið sáldraðist
í vitin

Hvassar tennur
stefndu að rósunum
á brjósti þínu

The sawdust was sprinkled
into nose and mouth

Sharp teeth
made for the roses
on your breast

Þá birtist
boxarinn

brá upp hnefunum

ólmum úlfum
sem rifu í sig
hvað sem fyrir varð

Dýr
alin til dráps

Enter then
the boxer

raised his fists

ravenous wolves
which bolted down
everything in their path

Beasts
reared for slaughter

Styggð
komst að
trúðunum

Bylur laukst
að baki þeim

A frenzy
seized
the clowns

The storm ceased
behind them

Þú steigst
upp úr kistunni

hálli sem hörpuskel

Snjórinn
eitruð aska
féll á hár þitt

You rose
from the coffin

that slippery scallopshell

The snow
poisoned ashes
fell onto your hair

Boxarinn
bauð þér heim
Þú gast ekki
annað en elt

The boxer
asked you home with him
You could not help
but follow

Myrkrið kvíslaðist
í konu og mann

Þú með sveipi
í ljósu hári
hann með lið
á margbrotnu nefi

nýstiginn
úr hringnum

The darkness forked
into a woman and man

You with a curl
in fair hair
he with a curve
on a much-broken nose

newly returned
from the ring

Í þrílyftu timburhúsi
átti hann sér

afdrep

In a three-storeyed house
of timber

was his lair

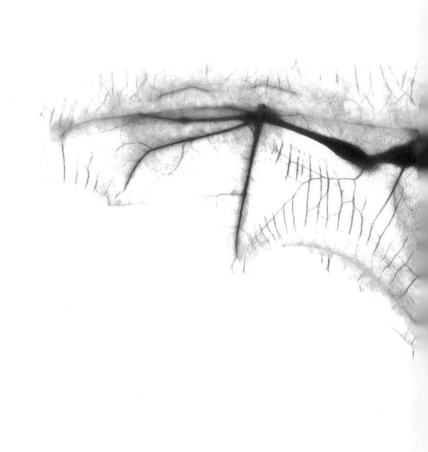

Gnestir
knúðu dyra

Þú leist út
í leit að
norðurljósum
en þau voru
hulin skýjum

There were creaking noises
knocks on the door

You looked out
in search of
the northern lights
but they were
hidden by clouds

Að baki þér
boxarinn
kreppti hnefann
um svipuskeftið

Myrkusstjórinn
var mættur
að tyfta þig og aga

augun dimmir gígar

Behind you
the boxer
clenched his fist
round the whip-handle

The darcus ringmaster
had come
to chasten and tame you

his eyes dark craters

Hann villti þig
með rúnum
rændi brauðmolunum
úr lófa þínum
svo þú rataðir ekki
um borgarskóginn

Hafi hann sjálfur
gengið heill til skógar
var engum vogandi
inn í þann myrkvið

He gulled you
with runes
stole the crumbs
from your palm
so you lost your way
in the urban forest

If he had walked there
hale and hearty
none would dare enter
that gloomy wood

Þú veittir því
ekki athygli
fyrr en of seint
að húsið sökk

Vatnið ýrðist
milli fjala
fossaði inn
um glugga

Þú greipst
í boxarann

You paid   hönd þín
no heed   lauf í lófa hans
to the house sinking
until too late

The water sprayed
between boards
cascaded in
through windows

You grabbed hold
of the boxer

your hand
a leaf in his palm

Hann þekkti rastirnar
sem réðu ferðinni

Þú lærðir
að streitast ekki
á móti

Þið lokuðuð
augunum
lyftust upp

He knew which way
the currents were tending

You learned
not to struggle
against them

You both closed
your eyes
you were lifted up

Sólfarið reif sig laust
og ruddist yfir fjörugrjótið

þríarma möstrin
teygðu sig
til himna

beinaber skrokkurinn
skreið út
á næturhafið

Borgin
slegin nóttu
hvarf í kóf

The Sun Voyager broke free
careered across the stony beach

the three-armed masts
reached upwards
to the heavens

the skeletal hull
slithered forth
onto night-wrapped sea

The city
overcome by night
vanished into drifting snow

Daginn eftir
vöknuðuð þið
á grúfu á gólfinu

stirð eins og
drumbar

The next day
you both woke up
face down on the floor

stiff as
logs of wood

Örlöglaus
skreiddust þið
á fætur
að leita vista

Þið höfðuð
numið nýtt land

Fateless
you dragged yourselves
to your feet
seeking provisions

You had settled
a new land

Einn var þó
fyrir á fleti

frumbygginn
ég

There was however
one there before you

the aboriginal
myself

Ég hef
fylgst með þér

Stundum er ég hundur
bundinn við bekk
stundum maður
með hófa
og hatt sem slútir
ofan í þrútið andlit

I've followed you
closely

Sometimes I'm a dog
tied to a bench
sometimes a man
with hooves
and hat pulled down
onto a swollen face

Það er ekki grein
sem lemst við
bárujárnið
heldur ég
að sverfa svartar klær

svo ég fái
grafið mig inn
að hjartanu

It is not a branch
beating against
the corrugated iron
it is me
filing black claws

so that I may
dig myself in
to the heart

Ég dæli í það
bleki

Breyti ykkur
í byttur

I pump ink
into it

I turn the two of you
into die-hard drinkers

Þú gekkst
í myrkusinn

Þegar svipan
skipaði þér
að stinga höfði
í ljónsgin
og finna úfinn
kitla á þér hvirfilinn
gerðirðu það

Into the darcus ring
you went

When the whip
made you
stick your head
in the lion's mouth
and feel its uvula
tickle the crown of your head
you did so

Þegar svipan
skipaði þér
að dansa á línu
fuglafit milli
fingra minna
gerðirðu það

Borgin slegin
nóttu
hvarf í kóf

When the whip
made you
dance on a tightened
thread between
my fingers
you did so

The city
overcome by night
vanished into drifting snow

Þetta hlaut
að fara
illa

Hlaut

This had to have
an evil
end

Just had to

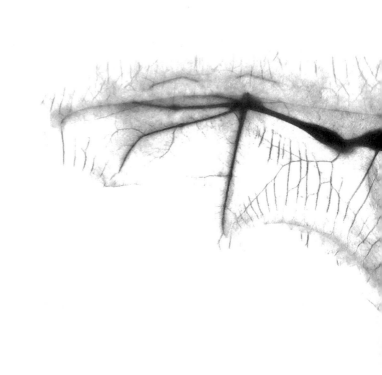

Öldugjálfur
yfirgnæfir brestina
í himnafestingunni

Nóttin flæðir að
fyllir götur og tún
streymir inn stíga
stefnir upp Holtið
færir kirkjuna á kaf

A lapping of waves
bursts through the cracks
in the vault of heaven

Night is flooding
fills streets and gardens
finds paths for its flow
heads up to Thingholt
submerges the church

Húsið rís upp
af hafsbotni
ryðst upp úr klöppinni

Bárujárnið
bylgjast í straumi

The house rises up
from the sea's bed
pushes up through the rocky ground

The corrugated iron
billows in the current

Mín er borgin
myrk sem blý

Ég syndi um
sokkinn bæ
sveigi hjá
fljótandi köttum

Mine is the city
dark as lead

I swim around
a sunken town
passing floating cats
as I go

Líð að ljósi
í risi hússins

Þaðan berst
þungur dynur
eins og hjarta slái
í viðnum

I glide towards the light
in the house's attic

From which there is borne
a booming noise
as of a heart beating
in the very timber

Vængir brjótast
úr baki mér
svört segl
strengd milli
tálgaðra tinda

Ég stíg
upp úr vatninu
vind mér inn

Wings sprout
from my back
black sails
pulled tight between
carved peaks

I rise up
out of the water
turn quickly in

Þú hangir föst
í fléttuðu hengi

Loftfimleikastúlka
hefur hrapað til bana
með línuna vafða
um hálsinn

þræði örlaganorna

You hang suspended
in a plaited rack

A girl acrobat
has fallen to her death
with the tightrope woven
round her neck

the threads of the fates

Brostin augun
kringd bláu mari

Svipurinn ber vott
um að þér hafi
borist svar
við spurningu sem
þú þorðir aldrei
að spyrja

Fyrir þitt litla líf
verður ekkert gert

Bulging eyes
ringed by blue bruising

Your expression bears witness
that you have received
an answer
to the question
you never dared
to ask

For your little life
nothing can be done

Boxarinn
sefur svefni
hinna ranglátu

djúpum
og draumlausum

The boxer
sleeps the sleep
of the unjust

a deep
dreamless sleep

Ég lýt niður að þér
svo varir mínar
nema við þínar

I bend down towards you
so my lips
touch yours

Tunga mín
leikur um
luktan svip
þreifar undir
þung augnlokin

sleiki út
slokknaðar stjörnur
botnlaus svarthol
blasa við

My tongue
slurps around
an expressionless face
feels its way beneath
the heavy eyelids

I lick away
extinguished stars
bottomless black holes
stare forth

Ég sleiki
tungum tveim
beittir broddar
ryðjast inn í vitin
vinda sig
um kúpuhvolfið

skafa út
heilan heim

I lick
with two tongues
their spiky tips
push into mouth and nose
twist their way around
the cranial vault

scrape out
an entire world

Ég veit
hvað höfuð þitt vó
en þekki ekki
síðustu hugsunina
sem barðist þar um
eða hverjum hún var ætluð

I know
what your head weighed
but do not know
the last thought
which struggled there
or for whom it was meant

Lungun veg ég
í lófum mínum
belgi þau út með blæstri

hlusta á loftið
seytla út aftur

Fyrir þitt litla líf
fæst ekkert lengur

I weigh the lungs
in the palms of my hands
inflate them by blowing

then listen to the air
making its escape

Of your little life
there is nothing left

Ég losa þig
úr fléttunni
legg þig út af
læt sem þú sofir

Sá sem er
á himnum
horfir tungleygur
til okkar

aðhefst ekkert

I release you
from entanglement
I lay you down
I pretend you are asleep

The one
up above
watches us
moon-eyed

does nothing

Það fjarar
undan nóttinni

Ég tek þig
í fangið
þen út seglin
hef mig á loft

Night is left
high and dry

I take you
in my arms
let the sails unfurl
raise myself aloft

Hár þitt
hvít ull
leggst yfir
öxl mína

Your hair
white wool
falls over
my shoulder

Janúardagur
drífur að mjöll

Nú spora
kettir út
spánnýja fönn

Aldrei sýna fuglarnir
himinbreiðunni
sömu óvirðingu

A January day
brings snow aplenty

Cats now
leave tracks
on the freshly-formed drifts

The birds never show
the flatland of heaven
the same disrespect

Ég færi þig
eineygða guðinum
þeim sem skapaði
manninn í sinni mynd
og engist nú af eftirsjá

I convey you
to the one-eyed god
the one who created
man in his image
and now writhes with regret

Hann sér um sína
kemur þér fyrir
í fallegu leiði

stráir föl yfir

Nafnið þitt
skrifað með
gylltu letri
á lágan stein

He looks after his own
settles you
in a beautiful grave

sprinkles snow over it

Your name
inscribed
in gilded lettering
on a pillow of stone

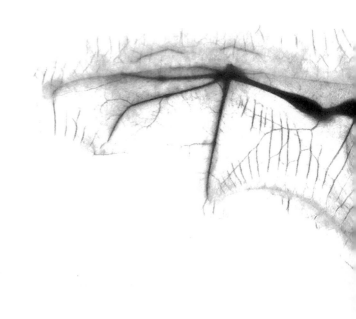

Vor tekur við
svo sumar með
sólríkum dögum

Þegar vetur
snýr aftur
er hann hálfu verri
en fyrr

Norðurljós nötra
í borg varga
og sorgar

Spring follows winter
then comes summer
with days of sunshine

When winter
returns
it is worse by half
than before

The northern lights tremble
in a city of villains
and ill-omen

Stræti lostin
frosti

dimmhvítum degi

Streets stricken
by frost

by dim light of day

Gestur birtist
í hálfsokknu húsinu
eins og sendur
eftir bendingu
úr gömlu handriti

Hvít málning
lekur niður kinnarnar

Augun sokkin
í svertu

A guest appears
in the half-sunken house
as if sent in pursuance
of instructions found
in an ancient manuscript

White paint
drips down his cheeks

His eyes are sunk
in blackness

Hann vill komast
í iðuna
en boxarinn
vísar honum burt

He seeks to gain entry
to the whirlpool
but the boxer
waves him away

Þá dregur gesturinn
fram hnífa

Einn af öðrum
hæfa þeir
boxarann í brjóstið
spretta upp
húð
skera á æð
og sin

Straumurinn litast
draumrauður

Then the guest
pulls out knives

Which one after the other
lunge
at the boxer's breast
open up
the flesh
cut at vein
and sinew

Red as in dreams
is the flow of blood

Myrkustjaldið
fellur

Trúðar berast nú aðeins
martraða á milli

The darcus's big top
falls

Clowns now feature
only in nightmares

Boxaranum er
holað niður
hjá ættingjum

Nafn hans hvergi nefnt

Slík eru örlög
svarthjartaðra manna

The boxer
is dug in
alongside relatives

His name nowhere inscribed

Such is the fate
of black-hearted men

Það er stutt
milli leiða ykkar
rétt svo að taki því
fyrir hrafnana
að lofa græsku grafarans
þegar þeir flögra á milli

It's a short distance
between your graves
giving little time
for the ravens
to praise the digger's malice
as they flutter between them

Börn hafa
grafið snjókarla
úr fönn

Grjóteygir
standa þeir vörð
um garðinn

Children have
made snowmen
from drifted snow

stony-eyed
they stand guard
over the garden

Ég minnist þín
þegar jólaljós og
janúar renna í eitt

Ég minnist þín
þegar stjörnurnar
myljast niður af himninum
svo brotin ganga
upp í blóðrisa þófana á mér

Ég minnist þín

I remember you
when Christmas lights
and January merge

I remember you
when the stars
shatter down from heaven
and their shards jab
at my blood-stained paws

I remember you

Vonandi var
einhver hjá þér
þegar þú vaknaðir

leiddi þig
yfir mýrarnar

las þér
vætuskúf í vönd
loðvíði
stör

Vonandi
fékkstu allt
sem þú áttir
skilið

Let us hope there was
someone beside you
when you awoke

led you
over the marshlands

gathered for you
a sheaf of spike-rushes
woolly willow
sedge

Let us hope
you received everything
you deserved

Borgin
slegin nóttu

Drottinn
dregur sig
í hlé

Augað blindað
bólsturskýi

The city is
stricken by night

The Lord
takes his leave

His eye blinded
by a low wad of cloud

Enn djarfar
fyrir svip mínum
í hélu götunnar

Strekkingurinn
stígur í vænginn við mig

sækir í sig
veðrið

Even now my shape
can be glimpsed, etched
in the street's hoarfrost

the strong wind
strokes my wing in courtship

gathers strength
into itself

Kuldinn
heggur sér leið
gegnum
Skuggahverfið

The cold
hacks itself a path
through the Shadow district

Ég spandéra ekki
fleiri dögum hér
en ég þarf

lyfti mér til flugs

hverf í kóf

I spend
no more days here
than I need

raise myself in flight

vanish into drifting snow

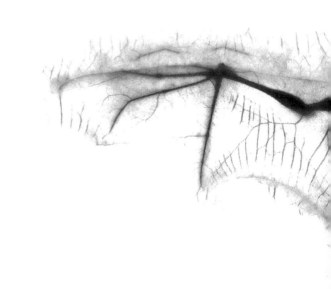

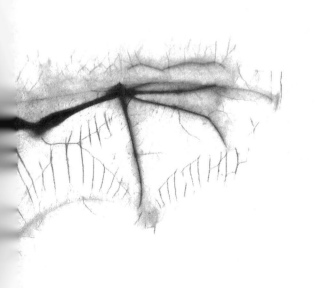

Icelandic Pronunciation
an approximate guide

In this bilingual edition of *Drápa*, readers are strongly advised to compare the translation with the original Icelandic. Those readers who know Icelandic will soon find that the translation is not a literal one, and cannot always be matched word for word with the original. But whether they know Icelandic or not, readers will gain much from reading the poem aloud in the original language. With this in mind I give below a brief approximate guide to Icelandic pronunciation, covering only those points that are relevant to a reading of *Drápa*; it makes no claim to overall coverage.

NB: The stress should always be on the first syllable of the word.

Vowels without acute accents over them are pronounced very much as in English, except that:
    a falls somewhere between the standard English pronunciations of *father* and *fat*
    a followed by *ng* (as in e.g. *fanga*, p. 39) is pronounced like *ow* in English *how*
    i and *y* are pronounced as in English *hit*
    i (or *y*) followed by *ng* or *gi* (as in *stingandi*, p. 42, *nýstiginn*, p. 56) is pronounced like *ee* in *seen* (for the pronunciations of *g*, see below)
    u is pronounced as in *put* (not as in *but*)
    æ is pronounced like English *eye*

ö like *oe* in *Goethe*

The diphthong *au* is pronounced like *eui* in French *feuille* (not like *au* in German *Haus*)

The diphthongs *ei* and *ey* are pronounced like *ay* in English *day*

Vowels with acute accents are pronounced as follows:
á like English *ow* in *how*
é like *ye* in *yes*
í and *ý* like *ee* in *seen*
ó like English *oh*
ú like *oo* in *moon*

As for the consonants, the two letters least familiar to novices, *þ* and *ð*, are pronounced as follows:
þ like *th* in English *thin*
ð like *th* in English *that*

The consonants *b, d, h, k, m, t, v,* single *l* and single *n* are pronounced much as in English.

f is pronounced:

(1) like *f* in English *father* at the beginning of a word (*fallið*, p. 29) and before *t* (*aftur*, p. 42) or *s* (*hnífsoddar*, p. 29, *ufsagrýlur*, p. 34)

(2) like English *p* before *l* or *n* (*sveifluðu*, p. 43; *stefnir*, p. 75)

(3) otherwise, like English *v* in the middle or the end of a word (*lófa*, p. 33, *hurfu*, p. 35, *kóf*, p. 64, *hafið*, p. 38, *nef*, p. 47, *ofan*, p. 38), except that

(4) it is all but lost if followed by *nd* or *nt* (*stefndu*, p. 51, *nefnt*, p. 101)

g (never pronounced as in English *George*) is pronounced:

(1) like English *g* (as in *girdle, green, agnostic,* etc.) at the beginning of a word or word-element (*götur,* p. 29, *ufsagrýlur,* p. 34, *gneistum,* p. 43, *yfirgnæfir,* p. 75)

(2) after *n* as in English *anger, linger, hunger* (not as in *hanging, singing, hung*) (*héngu,* p. 34, *fanga,* p. 39, *stingandi,* p. 42, *tungum,* p. 85), except when the combination *ng* occurs before a consonant, in which case the *g* is all but lost to the ear (*strengd,* p. 79, *kringd,* p. 81, *hringnum,* p. 56, *fingra,* p. 72, *ranglátu,* p. 82)

(3) before *l* within a word, like *g* in English *ugly* (*marglit,* p. 30, *athygli,* p. 62, *fuglafit,* p. 72), though the *g* is all but lost in the consonant clusters *naglför,* p. 50, *sigldu,* p. 43

(4) like *g* in Spanish *luego* when occurring singly after a vowel (*og,* p. 29, *Flugvél,* p. 30, *lagði,* p. 33, *stigu,* p. 45, *vogandi,* p. 61, *örlöglaus,* p. 66, *ég,* p. 35), or after *au* (*augun,* p. 60), *ei* (*steigst,* p. 54) or *ey* (*teygðu,* p. 64), though not if immediately followed by *i*, in which case it is pronounced like *y* in *yes* (*slegin,* p. 64, *sagið,* p. 51, *nýstiginn,* p. 56, *borgarskóginn,* p. 61, *Daginn,* p. 65, *grjóteygir,* p. 103), and it is all but lost after *á, ó,* if followed by *a* or *u* in the next syllable (*skógar,* p. 61, *slógu,* p. 45, *lágan,* p. 93)

(5) otherwise in general like English *g* (*borgin,* p. 77, *borgarbúar,* p. 38, *bólgið,* p. 47, *margbrotnu,* p. 56, etc.)

gg is pronounced as in English, though somewhat more emphatically

hv may be pronounced either as *kv* (as in *akvavit*), or with full value given to the *h* and the *v* as each of these two letters is pronounced in English: *hvíldi*, p. 35, *hvarf*, p. 64

j is pronounced like English *y* in *yes*

ll is pronounced like *ttl* in *settler*, e.g. *fallið*, p. 29, *mjöll-inni*, p. 29, *fellur*, p. 31, etc., except that in the cases of *gylltir*, p. 46, *villti*, p. 61, and *gylltu*, p. 93, it is pronounced like English *guilty* with the tip of the tongue raised to the back of the upper front teeth

mm is pronounced as in English, though with the sound somewhat protracted

nn is also pronounced much as in English, except that when following *ei* (as in *Einn*, p. 67) it sounds like *tn* in *Etna*

p and *pp* are pronounced as in English, though not before *s* or *t*, where they are pronounced like *f* (1), above (*greipst*, p. 42, *steypti*, p. 44, *gleypti*, p. 47, *kreppti*, p. 60)

r is more strongly trilled than in English, so that *rn* sounds somewhat like *tn* (*Stjörnur*, p. 29, *dúfurnar*, p. 34, *kirkju-turninum*, p. 36, *Snjókorn*, p. 37, *Trúðarnir*, p. 49, etc.)

s should be pronounced as in *house*, not as in *rose*

Rory McTurk

Biographical Notes

GERÐUR KRISTNÝ was born in 1970 and brought up in Reykjavík and graduated in French and Comparative Literature from the University of Iceland in 1992. She is now a full-time writer.

Gerður Kristný has published poetry, short stories, novels and books for children, and a biography *Myndin af pabba – Saga Thelmu* (Portrait of Daddy – Thelma's Story) for which she won the Icelandic Journalism Award in 2005.

Other awards for her work include the Children's Choice Book Prize in 2003 for *Marta Smarta* (Smart Martha), the Halldór Laxness Literary Award in 2004 for her novel *Bátur með segli og allt* (A Boat with Sail and All) and the West-Nordic Children's Literature Prize in 2010 for the novel *Garðurinn* (The Garden).

Her collection of poetry, *Höggstaður* (Soft Spot), was nominated for the Icelandic Literature Prize in 2007 and she then won the prize in 2010 for her poetry book *Blóðhófnir* (Bloodhoof). A bilingual edition of *Bloodhoof*, translated into English by Rory McTurk, was published by Arc Publications in 2012.

Gerður Kristný lives in Reykjavík but travels regularly around the world to present her work.

Rory McTurk graduated from Oxford in 1963, took a further degree at the University of Iceland, Reykjavík in 1965, and after teaching at the universities of Lund and Copenhagen, and then University College, Dublin, took up a post at Leeds University in 1978.

In addition to his two authored books, *Studies in Ragnars Saga Loðbrókar and its Major Scandinavian Analogues* (Oxford, 1991) and *Chaucer and the Norse and Celtic Worlds* (Aldershot, 2005), he has edited the *Blackwell Companion to Old Norse-Icelandic Literature and Culture* (Oxford, 2004), and co-edited, with Andrew Wawn, a volume of essays, *Úr Dölum til Dala* (From Dalir to the Dales) (Leeds, 1989) in commemoration of the Icelandic scholar Guðbrandur Vigfússon (1827-89). He has contributed editions of Old Norse works of literature to *A New Introduction to Old Norse, Part II, Reader*, 5th edition, ed. Anthony Faulkes (London, 2011) and to *Skaldic Poetry of the Scandinavian Middle Ages*, Vol. VIII, ed. Margaret Clunies Ross (Turnhout, 2017).

His publications also include two Icelandic saga translations, two book-length translations of scholarly works on Icelandic topics (one from Swedish, the other from Icelandic), numerous essays and articles, and translations (published in 2007 and 2015) of two novels by the Icelandic writer Steinunn Sigurðardóttir: *Tímaþjófurinn* (The Thief of Time) (Reykjavík, 1986) and *jójó* (Yo-yo) (Reykjavík, 2011).

GUÐNI ELÍSSON is Professor of Literature in the Faculty of Icelandic and Comparative Cultural Studies at the University of Iceland. His PhD in English Literature was on George Gordon, Lord Byron. Guðni has written on topics including film theory, the Gothic tradition, contemporary poetry, and climate change discourse. He is the founder of the environmental project Earth101.

ALDA BJÖRK VALDIMARSDÓTTIR is a Senior Lecturer in the Faculty of Icelandic and Comparative Cultural Studies at the University of Iceland. Her PhD in Comparative Literature is on Jane Austen's popularity in contemporary culture. Alda has written on topics such as the adaptation of literary models, celebrity studies, and contemporary fiction and poetry. She published her first volume of poetry in 2015 with Forlagið, Iceland's foremost publishing house.

ARC PUBLICATIONS
publishes translated poetry in bilingual editions
in the following series:

ARC TRANSLATIONS
Series Editor Jean Boase-Beier

'VISIBLE POETS'
Series Editor Jean Boase-Beier

ARC CLASSICS:
NEW TRANSLATIONS OF GREAT POETS OF THE PAST
Series Editor Jean Boase-Beier

ARC ANTHOLOGIES IN TRANSLATION
Series Editor Jean Boase-Beier

NEW VOICES FROM EUROPE & BEYOND
(anthologies)
Series Editor Alexandra Büchler

details of which can be found on the
Arc Publications website at
www.arcpublications.co.uk